My Little Golden
AIRPLANES

By Michael Joosten
Illustrated by Paul Boston

The editors would like to thank John Little, Assistant Curator
and Research Team Leader, the Museum of Flight, for his assistance
in the preparation of this book.

☙ A GOLDEN BOOK • NEW YORK

Educators and librarians, for a variety of teaching tools, visit us at
RHTeachersLibrarians.com
Library of Congress Control Number: 2018956095
ISBN 978-0-525-58182-6 (trade) — ISBN 978-0-525-58183-3 (ebook)
Printed in the United States of America
10 9 8 7 6 5 4 3 2 1

For many thousands of years, people watched birds and wondered what it would be like to fly. And for hundreds of years, artists and inventors tried to find a way for people to do it.

A little more than a hundred years ago, their dreams finally came true.

In 1903, two brothers named Wilbur and Orville Wright built an airplane out of spruce wood and took it to Kitty Hawk, North Carolina, for a test flight.

For twelve seconds, the Wright brothers' plane flew ten feet off the ground. As the first people to get a powered plane into the air, the brothers made history—and changed travel forever.

It wasn't long before air shows, also called flying circuses, were presented to thousands of curious people.

Bessie Coleman, the first African American woman to earn a pilot's license, performed daring stunts called aerobatics in some of these shows. She even parachuted to the ground to give the crowd an extra thrill! No wonder her nicknames were Queen Bessie and Brave Bessie.

One of the most famous moments in aviation history took place in 1927. Charles Lindbergh set out to become the first pilot to fly solo, nonstop, across the Atlantic Ocean. He had even decided to fly without a radio or a parachute so his plane would weigh less and his fuel would last longer.

Many people thought he was foolish to attempt such a dangerous flight. But after flying for thirty-three and a half hours, Lindbergh's plane, *The Spirit of St. Louis,* landed safely in Paris. Lindbergh instantly became an international hero, and even had a dance named after him—the Lindy Hop!

Five years later, Amelia Earhart became the first woman to complete a solo flight across the Atlantic Ocean. For this feat, the United States Congress awarded her the Distinguished Flying Cross.

Amelia soon had a new goal: to become the first person to fly around the world. But in 1937, she and her plane vanished over the Pacific Ocean. Her plane has never been found.

When the United States entered World War I in 1917, its military began to use airplanes for dangerous combat missions.

World War II saw even more fighter planes in the skies, such as the Hawker Hurricane, the Supermarine Spitfire, the Republic P-47D Thunderbolt, and the North American Aviation P-51D Mustang.

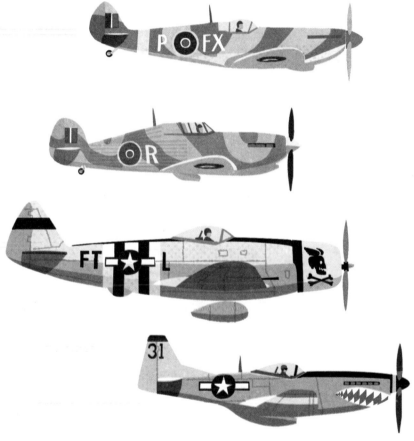

To help boost pilot morale, cartoons, famous characters, and even shark's teeth were often painted on the planes' noses.

The first jet-powered airplane designed to carry passengers, the de Havilland Comet, was built in 1949. The plane's engines were placed inside the wings, rather than under them, so it could fly faster.

Since then, airplane engines have been positioned under the wings or on the tail—and some are in both places. Jet planes can fly up to 50,000 feet in the air, so they require a special fuel that won't freeze in the cold temperatures experienced at that height.

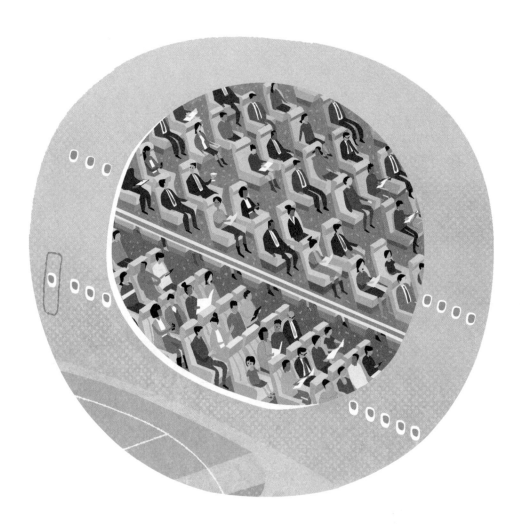

The largest passenger plane is the Airbus A380. It has an upper deck, can carry up to 850 people, and can fly for more than seventeen hours without stopping to refuel!

The fastest passenger plane ever designed was the Concorde. It could hold as many as one hundred passengers, fly up to 1,350 miles per hour, and get from New York City to Paris in only three hours!

But tickets for the Concorde were too expensive for most people, so it was taken out of service in 2003.

Did you know that some planes can land on water? Once used for difficult rescue missions, they're still used to fly passengers into hard-to-reach areas near bays or lakes.

The U.S. Navy has flown many different kinds of planes over the years. Some, such as F/A-18s, even take off and land on ships called aircraft carriers!

Because the runway on an aircraft carrier is only about 500 feet long, the F/A-18 has a special tailhook to help it land. The tailhook catches on a steel wire that is stretched across the ship's deck, which helps the plane stop quickly.

The B-2 Spirit, also known as the Stealth Bomber, was specially designed to be nearly undetectable on enemy radar. It can also refuel in midair, thanks to another plane called a tanker aircraft. The tanker aircraft delivers fuel through a thick tube that extends from the back of the plane.

Have you ever heard of the Blue Angels? This special group of pilots is made up of U.S. Navy and Marine Corps aviators. They fly F/A-18s that can travel up to 1,190 miles per hour! The Blue Angels perform for huge crowds, creating daring formations and doing exciting midair tricks, such as high-speed passes, loops, and barrel rolls.

In the future, technology will bring us planes
that fly higher and faster than ever before . . .

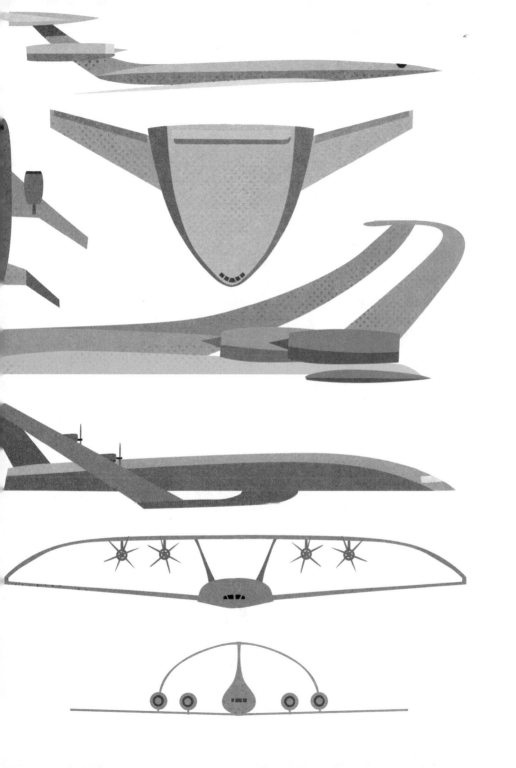

. . . and maybe *you* will fly one of them!